LOVE HOUSE

LOVE HOUSE

Poems by
Frank X Walker

Accents Publishing • Lexington, Kentucky • 2023

Printed in the United States of America

Accents Publishing
Editor: Katerina Stoykova-Klemer
Cover Photo by Shauna Morgan

Library of Congress Control Number: 2023947051
ISBN: 978-1-961127-03-6
First Edition

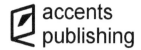

Accents Publishing is an independent press for brilliant voices. For a catalog of current and upcoming titles, please visit us on the Web at

www.accents-publishing.com

CONTENTS

For my sister, Wanda Marie Walker.

LOVE HOUSE

Even when we were playing house,
the home we were building in our hearts
was made of air, poems, books, and art.
That's all we needed, until we peeled back

the covers and saw our children sitting there
waiting to be fed, hugged, nurtured, coached,
and praised. Where we lived was too far apart,
too suburban, too complicated   to last.

Blending households, the old-fashioned way,
with a whisk, wasn't enough. We folded in family
and friends to thicken the batter. We created
something sweet and new from scratch. Took

all those promises and built us a house, in an artists'
village, with yellow doors and tall built-in selves.

OUR LITTLE RED COUCH

… is not the wasteland,
sanctum, or temporary bed
of the offending spouse
in a marital dispute,

but the port of reentry,
a pillowy Switzerland,
more therapist office
than courtroom.

It is not unlike a small church
where two or more gathered
together in His or Her name
can lay hands on each other,

seek absolution,
lay burdens down
before ascending the stairs
to Heaven.

WHY I HATE MORNINGS

It's not the premature waking,
the separation

from technicolor dreams,
jump starting a new to-do list,

or the sound of alarms going off.
It's the thought of surrendering

the perfect comfort and warmth
that I've spent all night chasing.

DAYLIGHT SAVINGS TIME

Winter's not over until my third trip back
from the car wash and the steady increase
of winged couples, chasing and flirting,
remind me that the birdseed is getting low.

It's not really spring until already-fat robins are
hopping through the yard taking inventory of
all the places the lawn mower missed.

It's not time to change the clocks until morning
light's attempt to sneak in the window
before we wake, triggers the motion detector
activating a chorus of chirping in the trees.

SERIAL MONOGAMIST

Don't ask me for marital advice.
I've failed at "death do us part"
four times.

The first time, we were pregnant.
I misunderstood what mama meant
by "the right thing,"
so I said I do, but I didn't.

On my second try, I took a trophy wife
in a soulless game
of *Keeping up with the Joneses*,
but I only missed her when she was gone.

My third wife felt guilty for abandoning
her little boy, so she let a petulant,
teenage-him move in with no rules
and no consequences.
Our unity & bliss became collateral damage.

Number four valued money above everything,
even *my* kids. I fell out of lust
at our one and only budget summit.
For closure, I met her at the bank.

When number five gives in to anger,
she is quick to remind me
I am the common denominator.
Four different women couldn't all be wrong.
That the problem is obviously   me.

EDITOR

You smooth out my misspelled wrinkles
in the sheets.

You reorder the entire opening paragraph
when I finish loading the dishwasher.

You point out the semicolon of sleep I missed
in the boy's eye after I wash his face.

You are the original AutoCorrect and editor,
headmaster and mistress of this finishing school.

Who knew the *MLA Handbook*
devoted a whole chapter to toilet seats?

WHEN I KNEW I WAS WOMAN

for Shauna

I memba dat time
I got sick real bad

Den mi twins got sick
Den dey fadah got sick

Den, I couldn't be sick
no more.

SELFIE: SONS

It's an always looking backwards
never forward, despite charges
that I "spit him out."

I have looked for him there but never
found him, only you and more and more
of you with each passing glance.

Though he is the spitting image of me
and I of you, mirrors clearly don't tell
the future. They only whisper our past.

MALIBU JACK'S

for Kumasi

I.

The parking lot is nearly full.
Carloads of sugared-up kids are racing
towards the entrance of the indoor theme park,
a warehouse-sized sensory wonderland for kids.

My son is out of his coat as soon as we walk in.
The buzz of the swarm of bodies
keeps him tethered long enough for me to pay
for an all-day pass, skip the go-karts, laser tag,
miniature golf, arcade games, bowling, food,
and head straight for the mecca, Bounce Beach.

The children are already delirious with joy,
but the parents and guardians are palpably sad.
It's another cold Kentucky public school Spring Break
and this is as close as most of us will get to Florida.

II.

There are two kinds of guardians at the beach:
amateurs and veterans. The novices will try to keep
their charges in sight, a Herculean task
even for parents dressed in athletic gear and shoes.
In addition to the large inflatable bouncing rooms,
there is a multi-level, kid-sized, gigantic rat maze
attached to miniature playrooms, with mesh partitions,
climbing walls, rope obstacle courses, swinging rings,
punching dummies, and a variety of giant slide exits all
attached to an overhead tunnel that connects
one side of the play area to another.

The more seasoned among us will station ourselves
near the middle, eye level to the bouncy room doors,
across from the logical paths in between,
our heads on a swivel, in view of the main exit,
in case somebody tries to steal our kids.
Here we can also entertain ourselves counting
the anxious faces of parents of lost kids,
while side-eyeing adults bent over cell phones,
as if we weren't raised by a helicopter-less generation
who left us outside all day, unsupervised, who parented by
confidently throwing us into the deep end.

III.

My son is all about the castle-themed bounce room
until the bubblegum rave erupts into a mosh pit.
And he's already not that social with strangers.

Too many kids here are rude, aggressive, unapologetic,
and seemingly entitled.

I pretend that I can match the adults to their wards
as an anxious tearful wail unleashes mass panic
with cries of "I can't find my mommy!"

I'm the only Black man here. All the women smile
every time the brown boy with a sunburst of hair
bounces up to high-five me before disappearing again.

A sour-faced kid is pounding away at a dummy
with all his might. At least three adults are huddled
over sobbing puddles of kids.

Mine bounces til he's dizzy. He climbs everything,
spins in circles and squeals with joy between check-ins.

I consume myself with imagining what kind of grownups
they will become. I wonder how much playground etiquette,
or lack thereof, will survive adulthood. None of them
are worried about tomorrow. I wish I could do the same.

IV.

I admit it. I'm a little bit judgy with people.
I make unsound assumptions based on ignorance.

I'm reminded of how ridiculous that is when the child
with Down's Syndrome, not the oversized bully
who knocked down my kid, is swept up
into the overly-tattooed arms and neck
of the unsmiling man classified in my head as a thug.

And doubly so after that same lil' bully said yes ma'am
and grabbed his shoes when the pint-sized ol' lady
sitting next to me stopped smiling and barked,
"Now! I told you five minutes ten minutes ago."

LET THEM BEE

for the George Washington Carver STEM Academy for Boys

To call them a swarm is to at once deny
their warmth and sweetness. They buzz
around each other, zoom across the open
field, and make a beeline for the playground.

They land on and cover every inch of the slides,
the swings, and the seesaw equipment.
They crawl through the giant plastic tunnel
as if searching for the honeycomb.

Even the smallest of them evokes so much
unwarranted fear in others,
as if their would-be exterminators don't know or
care that only the females carry stingers.

Let them find their way. Let them grow and learn.
Let them be beautiful Black and Brown boyz.

KUMASI AT FIVE

My mother reared sons
on the straight and narrow,
too afraid to not do the right thing,
in a pinch.
So well-raised, we would never
get in trouble with the law.

It should be too soon for the talk.
My son is only five.

But we were born in a place
where our skin is a crime.
And Faith and prayers were the only
real protection we ever had.

She couldn't teach us how to survive
a chance encounter with police,
just about the need to avoid one.
By the time I was old enough to drive,
I heard every Black mother's warning
whenever I got behind the wheel.

It should be too soon for the talk.
My son is only five.

I had done nothing wrong when
I was pulled over the first time,
but I was still wringing wet
before I rolled down the window.

She wanted boys who were compliant,
too polite to mouth off at police.
Like her, I want my boy   alive.

But it should be too soon for the talk.
My son is only five.

SET POINT

"Start where you are. Use what you have.
Do what you can."
—Arthur Ashe

Arthur forever opened the Open
when he took down
a different bull, Connors,
but his brother Johnnie's sacrifice
—a second tour of Nam
allowed him the privilege
of serving his country
on the clay court.

It was 1968.
They were silencing decent,
forever quieting loud voices.
Like Jackie Robinson before him
he did not strut to the finish line,
yet he arrived with his dignity intact.
He showed us other ways to win.
Taught all who would listen
that taking break point
ends the match
if you serve the ball
with a cannon
or with a subtle slice.

THE WILD

We thought the dense wooded area
separating the railroad tracks
from the projects was the wild.

The prison cell of grass comprising
our front and back yards
were as small as our concrete-floor rooms.

We grew up thinking the barbed wire
fence separating the haves from the have
nots, was there to protect us, not them.

When my sister was arrested for stealing
a 45, they treated her like it was a gun,
not a small vinyl record.

MEDITATIONS ON EASTER
for Wanda

My sister loved the Resurrection
more than we all loved Easter dinner.
She thought the chocolate bunny
blasphemous, though she insisted
on large-scale egg hunts for the kids,
even when we were down to two.
The Passion plays she wrote were epic.
She was the queen of dramatic flair.
Her trifling husband played himself
as a cruel Roman soldier. Her begotten son
owned his role as Satan. Her wooly-headed
Jesus made half the congregation squirm.
I can still hear her say, "Brother, this year,
I want you to build me a tomb.
—and I want a stone door that rolls away."

SELFIE: GHOST CIGARETTE

Staring at the corner of my lips
I see it. It's not really there, but I see smoke
every time I look for me, and see you instead.

I cannot not see it any time
I look at your/my/our crooked mouth.
I never indulged. Your two packs per day

was more than enough for both of us.
The nicotine called, or was it as close as you
could get to your father's smoke and smile?

SELFIE: LIGHT SABER

> "Luke, I am your father."
> —Darth Vader

More Sith than Jedi,
the storm trooper
slinking out of my brow

reminds me
that even if I eclipse
my father's

almost eighty years
—every day after forty
is closer to the dark side.

MOON WALK

for Kumasi

When I wake up on the dark side
of the moon and am teetering
at the very edge of space,
I know our son has entered our orbit.

Young planets launched off their axis,
fleeing night terrors,
often gravitate up the stairs
seeking the warmth of celestial bodies
like the one nestled next to mine.

Sometimes their rotating trajectory
complete with moons and Saturn-like rings
of feet, sharp knees, and elbows
is just too much for a dying star like me.

Sometimes this new planetary alignment
gives birth to solar flares
which pull him from the depths of sleep
with declarations
of "I need more space mom!"

The resulting ripple effect is me
in my astronaut's robe, peering out
at the cosmos, seeking solace in the pages
of a book, folded into the engine
of our starship, back at work, even earlier
than I had planned.

HYDROGEN PLUS POTASSIUM

If you've ever had ulcers,
acid reflux, or the runs,
then you know our stomachs
keep us alive,
that the heart is just a battery,
the brain a catalytic converter.

Your stomach is an engine.
Hydrochloric acid works like transmission fluid
monitoring more than your feelings
keeping you honest
with bicarbonates, the bufferer,
balancing your pH.

Your hard shell is on the inside.
It's not your thick skin.
Epidermis can't protect you
when you swallow the truth.

If you've ever heard a laugh so deep
you knew it could only come from *here*
or witnessed a body collapse
after getting sucker punched with bad news,
know this—

If you ain't got the stomach
for words,
don't even think about
being a poet.

HUNGER PAINS

I remember Miracle Whip sandwiches,
the sound a spoon makes
at the bottom of an empty bowl,
plucking out the swirling dead roach
after stirring the last of the sugar
into the Kool-Aid.

I recall the meatiness of the heels,
the end of a loaf of bread,
how far tap water and a good shaking
could stretch a gallon of milk,
and the welcome texture peelings
added to fried potatoes and onions.

Except for Sundays, meat came
out of a can.
More mouths than meals meant
wasting nothing, even the mysterious
parts wrapped in thin white paper
and stuffed inside discounted chicken
at the supermarket.

Choosing between the gizzard and liver
or nothing was always a tough choice.

We learned to enjoy the ghost meat
on a chicken neck, and snapping open
bones to suck out the marrow.
Escaping poverty is hard work and luck.
But you never forget how no money tastes.

SELFIE: SIEGE

Increasingly more salt
than pepper
they huddle, no

they surround
my lips
with plans to guard my smiles

like I do,
like he did, though mama
was always more generous.

THE OLFACTORY AGE

When I was child, Sonya and Karla smelled
like talcum powder and baby lotion.

I reeked of sweat, of summer, and outdoors.
Mama's hands held both bleach and Blue Magic.

Five girl heads, no relaxers, and one straightening
comb was another full-time job.

Each of them smelled like bubble gum
and burnt hair until iron invaded their hips.

I thought Mama's mama smelled of mothballs.
Now that I am gray, I know it was a stew of Epsom salts,

pork in her greens, high blood pressure pills, baking powder
based denture cleaner, fish oils and elixirs for memory

loss, Preparation H or generic witch hazel equivalents,
ointments for rheumatism and arthritis, and soap

that just cleaned. No more wasted money on *foolishness*.
No more effort spent on pretending to smell any younger.

PLEASE THROW THIS ONE BACK

When my older cousins light up
talking about how much
Aunt Faye, my mama, loved to fish,
I can't help but squinch my eyes
and feel like something was stolen from me.

My mind travels back, searching for conversations
and images of her and fish and hooks, her and worms
and poles, and all I get is Mama at the kitchen sink
scaling and cleaning somebody else's fresh catch,
or mama at Red Lobster stuffing herself with biscuits,
already salivating over the whiting she ordered.

I reach even further back than I know, searching for
the fissure that happened in our universe,
and I see a lifeless body being pulled out
of the bottom of Herrington Lake,
a skinny, breathless poor man's dolphin.

I see her reach all the way across to the other side
begging and pleading on its behalf.

Wailing at the fin of the Savior.
Offering tributes in song and a lifetime of sweat.
Agreeing to never go anywhere near water,
to never cast another hook, or even stare into the deep,
ever again, in exchange for the life of the catfish
with my father's face.

I reach back again and see traffic pile up behind us
when she stopped the car and refused to drive
over Chenault Bridge. I think about my greatest fears
and how I've never been on a cruise
or fished on the open water from inside a boat.

I reach back to her panic at the aquarium
when the floor ended, and I was suddenly suspended,
imitating Jesus, over a thin sheet of glass,
a makeshift manmade sea.
She looked down, then could not cross,
choosing instead to turn and retrace her steps
to the entrance. She never explained
what paralyzed her so. Never spoke of it again.

As this great unraveling continues to work itself out,
the drowning sensation I feel in my body over water
and bridges lets me know that all of it, even the parts
that I don't quite understand, are more than true,
especially this: I was too small to eat,
so, my mama begged the Godfish to throw me back.

SELFIE: MISSING PERSONS

Mama used to stare off like that.
Some place far away,
some place nicer and easier

I always thought.
But now,
catching myself looking for her

in my smile,
I am wondering not where
she went, but to whom.

DEAD WEIGHT

I.

You think I did the right thing?
she asked her sister
with whom she shared almost everything,
a week after she left us, then came back
because a voice on the other side
reminded her that she had one more task to do.

She wanted to go clean.
She needed to cast off her last burden, a yoke
too heavy to carry   into the afterlife.

She wanted to weigh nothing   at the end.

So, when he finally crept into the room,
two weeks after she entered hospice,
performing his most pitiful self
and expecting to explain
where all her money went,
he was caught off guard
by the only words she had to say.

Whose idea was this, he demanded,
as loud as he dared, lest he risk the sounds
of metallic rumblings from her brood
just an excuse for an ass whupping away.

It was mine, she said, more clearly
and with more pride than when she first said,
I do, before punctuating it with silence.

II.

Mr. finally come today, whispered her sister,
out of the corner of her mouth,
with the appropriate amount of cigarette smoke.

How she doing? her brother asked.

Oh, she's light   as a feather and smiling.

They both closed their eyes
and watched the cloud fade away.

CONTROLLED BURN

I can't stop thinking   about how
language fails us   at the end.

Why puffing on cigarettes
is called smoking
and not stage one cancer.

Why Keytruda is called medicine
and not embalming fluid.

Hospice is too close to hospital
yet not far enough away from
inhospitable.

Mis diagnos is just a clinical way
to say death is coming
even sooner than you think.

Nobody should have to tell us
it's a bad idea to try to inhale fire.
We don't have the internal organs
or constitutions of dragons.

Tobacco belongs on the shelf
next to rat poison,
same aisle as arsenic,
just above racism and lye.

Marl boro really means
mini mushroom cloud
Hiro shima
a filterless wildfire
—in your lungs.

DEATH RATTLE

Nobody slept. We just lay there stretched out
on the floor like we did when we were kids,
all lined up like sardines in the same twin bed.
We couldn't. Our ears were too full of the air

raid that followed the pronouncement of her
imminent death. But she bombed the small room
the whole night, the next day, and the next
refusing to relent, exhibiting the defiance
in a heart that was always the strongest thing about her.

There is no quiet now. Even miles away in the dark
searching for sleep on my own pillow I can still hear
her breathe. I can still see her body swell and jerk,
dragging me back, with a few of my siblings in tow,
praying for no more suffering   and safe passage,

waiting for the sound of her one last breath
—unable to separate it from our own.

SELFIE: BRIDGE

> "We will cross that bridge when
> we come to it."
>
> —Mama

The bridge of my nose reminds me
that she is always here, even now
—and that she always knew

where I'd look
for help when the soul crusher
and the bill collector

knocked at the same time
and there was no place else to hide.
She knew. She always knows.

INHERIT

My body remembering
my mother's stroke
is all my headaches are.

The anxiety I often feel
is just the weight of doubt
handcuffed to her hopes
and dreams.

My aching joints are callbacks
to all the hardwood and porcelain
she scrubbed

on her hands and knees.

I wear her guilt and sorrows.
Every worry line and stomach
knot represents my inheritance.

We don't stand on the shoulders
of those that came before us.
We swim in the river of their fears.

AT SIXTY-ONE

An attention-seeking, rogue white diva in my right brow
waves at me from the mirror when I lean in to check
the length of the choir in my nostrils.

I often catch pains in odd places for no known reason
and hear myself saying way too often, I slept on it wrong
or that I simply stood up too fast.

Can't tell you how many times I've dropped pills
on the floor, shrugged my shoulders,
and just reached for another
not out of laziness, but out of fear
that if I bend that far down, I won't be able to get back up.

You know you're old if you put on a knee brace
to take out the trash
or when it's just too much trouble to make the correction
when strangers look at your son, smile,
and then tell you how cute your grandchild is.

SELFIE: IT'S NOT YOU, IT'S ME

My grumpy, too-early-in-the-morning
unrested face
looks more like you than me.

Bags under your eyes, crow's feet,
and deep frown lines
were your constant companions at this age.

Looking back at your retirement,
I now know that you weren't getting old.
You were just getting tired, like me.

CALL OF DUTY

At seventy-seven he denies it is his birthday,
accuses some invisible trickster
of counting behind his back,
claims he stopped counting many many years ago.

I tease him til he chuckles. I want to believe
he knew it was me before I called,
that he's been waiting all day to hear me perform
my part in our annual ritual.

The call lasts two minutes longer than it did when
he was the one who was fifty-four
and I was still weighting for
a thirty-one-year-old apology.

If I make it to seventy-seven, I hope he is still
here, that we have outgrown waiting
for forgiveness, and have finally discovered easier
ways to say, I love you.

SELFIE: CROSSING

If you can see these two new residents,
you're standing too close or
have been staring too long.

I've reached a new height of selfishness,
with a pair of solid white eyelashes,
grown in gently crossing each other,

like we did, like the two old men
we have become, a final gift from you
my own tribute X.

IN MY DREAM

An old Black man, much taller and stronger
than me with young Wole Soyinka hair,
is running down the center lane
of Main Street
right in front of the Kentucky Theater.

But I don't mean running
like   from something.
It is more like high-stepping,
on air, as if he was finishing
an easy 10K
and suddenly found enough energy
in a reserve tank
to sprint the final 300 yards
gobbling up everyone
who swam past him on the hill
with a look of victory in their eyes.

And I don't mean old
like the restored Theatre marquee above my head,
but odd-socks-and-don't-care old,
one-long-wild-silver-eyebrow old,
often-inappropriate-unfiltered-comment old,
never any shame just proud to have made it.

On my way to the obligatory
middle-of-the-night pee
I hold fast to this memory just behind smiling eyes.

I know I will search for him
in the exhausted throng beyond the finished line
when I follow this dream backwards.
I know he has much to teach me
—so I ask, will they remember how I ran the race,
or just how I finished?

SELFIE: POINTILLISM

These moles look more regal
on Morgan Freeman.
Finally finding their ways

from my family tree
to their appointed place
in the fallow field

beneath my eyes.
—they must know
they will be watered much.

AT GOVERNOR'S SCHOOL FOR THE ARTS

You wilted when you saw
her mixed-media sculpture,
a dark wooden house
with round bay windows,
a yellow door,
sawed in halves and dubbed,
Broken Home.

You ask her to talk about it.
She looked at you confused,
as if it was already crystal clear.
She didn't have the words,
and had already said
all she had to say and feel.

You missed the enthusiasm
she expressed
for the bridge she constructed
that connected the two jagged ends.
She was proud of all the extra time
and attention it took
to craft the delicate but sturdy thing
that holds both parts
of her life together.

You might still feel guilty for your part
in the fracture, but she took
the ugliest thing in her life
and made something beautiful
—a skill she learned from you.

ABUSE

Whiskey-breathed, heavy-handed men
of my grandfather's generation
smacked their loved ones around
as often as they changed their shirts.
Those women were among the first
to mask, to manufacture excuses
for bruises and busted lips. To explain
away deadly domestic differences.

Like bad husbands, we know Covid kills
every day, but we insist on ignoring
the truth, insisting we aren't afraid,
convincing each other that when
the final conflict inevitably occurs,
that it will be somebody else's loved one
at death's edge, not us, because
the pandemic is just misunderstood,
and it really and truly loves us.

NEOTERIC KAMA NO SUTRA

When pheromones, ignited by the promise
in her come-and-get-it smile, our kinetic skin,
and my hunger, sing to our son about how he got here
and why it all started, he finds a way to prove

umbilical cords are longer than desire. He cries
I just want you, and everything planned
or selfish and hard, in her, melts and is put on hold.
Something in the ether, in the dark or in our eyes

warns my mini me that another hymn could be made
in this moment. He remembers he does not share,
wedges his head into our groove, almost reprising
his birth. Like a wrestler needing to break a figure-four

leg lock or spill the Milk and Water Embrace,
he forces a submission, but we are patient and wait.

FEEL ME?

There will always be dissonance
between how you think
I think you felt
and how you actually feel
—unless you tell me.

TAKE ME

You say a little aggression
can be fun
but that you don't have rape
fantasies.
But after your wine,
my bourbon,
and too long
since the last time,
it's hard to tell the difference.

SLAVE NARRATIVE(S)

We both have read too much history,
know too much about trauma,
too much about generational pain
and ancestral memory
to ever get off   on bondage.

COTTON GIN FANS

Jack and Jill
went up the hill,
but Jill was pale
and Jack wasn't
which was problematic
for somebody at the top
which might explain
how Jack
fell down
and broke his crown
[both tooth
and access to throne]
and why Till came
tumbling afterwards.

HOCUS POCUS

The New York Times photo captures it all: the players on the almost all-white team from Iowa appear moored to the floor, while a Black girl on the almost all-black opposing team seemingly floats in the air, looks up and back at the basket, smiling, preparing to execute an acrobatic backwards no-look reverse bank layup.

In the background, the quietly adorned coach of the white team looks stupefied. And why wouldn't she? The commentators, the previous day's headlines, and all the sports prognosticators have already given her the crown.

Her squad was led inarguably by the best woman's player in the history of the game, a talented sharpshooter with NBA range who rarely missed. And they stormed out of the locker room, only 21 points down and put together a 15–2 run and were about to go out there and take the victory she had conjured up for them in her pregame speech.

But the scouting report didn't have any data on Black Girl Magic. She couldn't game plan against "wizardry!" How else could you explain a bench player hitting all five of her three-point shots and scoring 21 points in the first half or a "troubled" transfer scorching them with 19 down the stretch, when the whole world knew they had the best player on the court, a one-in-a-generation phenomenon?

This was supposed to be an easy win. They had already defeated the number one ranked, undefeated defending National Champions, hands down, the best team in the SEC, on the heels of her superstar's unheralded, already-legendary 41-point triple-double. And this was a much weaker team and a coach obsessed more with Mardi Gras than Xs and Os, whose best player was a tall skinny Black Barbie doll against her Valkyries.

This is why her players, their coaches, the legions of fans, the commentators, *Sports Illustrated* and *ESPN* all struggled to explain the unexplainable. It was not supposed to happen. But there it was. Captured in a frozen moment. On the front page. LSU Beat, no stunned, by obviously cheating, the ~~whiter~~ better team, with some kind of witchcraft, or did the obvious fouls this team had gotten away with all season suddenly lose their powers of invisibility? Ahhh, that explains it. It was the referees. It's always the referees.

MASTA D' STEALA

The truth about the history of bourbon
especially, when *they* say the secret
came from an "old family recipe,"
is that ol' Grand Dad likely owned the cook.

So, it ain't no different than colonels laying claim
to discovering the "thirteen herbs and spices"
that make the yardbird "finger lickin' good"
or Christopher   columbusing.

Jack Daniel told the truth about the African
source of the double filtration process,
but in Kentucky they give all the credit
to limestone in the water, before acknowledging
the Black hands of a cook or a cooper.

Truth is, somebody skilled enough to regulate
temperatures over an open fire, somebody who
knew cornmeal from cracked corn or grits,
and all about cooking   in vats and giant pots,

a body who knew how many heirloom kernels
it took to plant forty acres and feed the mule,
how many bushels to set aside as seed,

fingers that knew hoe & plow, plant & grow,
put mineral oil on the silk to stop the corn earworm,
knew how many stalks to let dry in the field
to be picked & husked after the silk turned brown.

Not shuck and jive, but shuck & shell—by hand,
to be ground or milled, barreled, shipped, and sold,
before using the cobs for kindling, dolls, or pipes
or for their private business in the outhouse.

A body who knew how much six-row barley
and when to add it,
to coax starch to fermentable sugars,
so that fruit or grain could be worshipped
as beer or wine on the way to being born again
as brandy or whiskey (bourbon in the bluegrass)

Every body knew a body with no land, no power,
no voice, no control, had   no say
over who say who is the master   distiller.

A PINCH OF SALT

None of us should remember,
but all of us do. A mouth full of tears
can trigger something bone deep,
even for those of us borne on this side,
deep like the taste of the cold waters
our foremothers rode in chains
across an ocean to get here.

Crying over our lot
don't do nothing but pickle the pain,
and rub brine into our open sores.

Salt helped keep us, allowed us
to pickle food, chase the rot off
a rare piece a meat or fish.
It helped wild greens kiss us back.

Throw a pinch over your shoulder
to ward off evil. Sprinkle down a hedge
to keep Ol' Scratch at bay.

The taste of salt is life.
Tasting salt is tasting our struggle.
We know to not use too much.
Even the Old Testament tells us,
too much salt—can kill.

JAYHAWKING

for Langston Hughes

In an era
when high yella dandies
were all ladies' men
in the open
and being a man's man
meant something different,
I wonder if well-put-together,
well-read, well-spoken,
and well-traveled
was enough camouflage
to shield you from additional
brutality
and disdain.

Dear Langston,
I hope you were as loved
in the dark
as John Brown was
feared in the light?

His good Lord
wanted us unshackled.
Yours   wanted all of us free.

DRIVE BUYS

People for whom
summer is a verb
creep down our inner-city
streets, hidden inside
dark, tinted Suburbans

appraising empty lots
and houses they imagine
they can steal
and flip for cheap.

We look for cover when
car windows slide down
and somebody takes aim
—points, clicks, and shoots.

ELVIS

put Gwen Christon's life story
in a song
almost fifty years ago,
except her lost love
was a grocery store, in Isom.
And the long walk
was more   of a swim.

He was right about the dozen towns.
He was right about the lonely back roads.

He must have seen Letcher County
and its surrounding hollers
under six feet of muddy water.

He must have had visions
of school buses only visible
by their roofs.

When he said,
love too strong to let you go,
he must have seen
the decades she would pour
into her IGA,
the people she would feed,
the community she would nourish,
and her own flood of tears
when the store was gone.

He was right about the old men
and the general store.

He was right
about the preacher man
and his prayers

to soothe her aching heart,
to reunite her with her love,
but he was mostly right
about the cold   Kentucky   rain.

EROSION

for Eastern Kentucky

When you remove
the tops of mountains,
when you disappear rich soil,
the rocks and the trees

> *Rain rain go away. Come again*
> *another day* … but not tonight
> and tomorrow and the next day
> and the next day

When you gut a body like a fish,
rip out it's backbone
to get to its coal black heart

> *It's raining men, hallelujah.*
> *It's raining men* … and cats and dogs
> and squirrels and rabbits
> and rattlesnakes and bears
> and wild turkeys and frogs
> and coons and buzzards

When the shelf is stocked
with food, but the bread
is under six feet of muddy water,
when there's food on the table,
but the table
is floating downstream

> *I'll go walking through*
> *with the rain in my shoes*
> *(rain in my shoes)*
> and in my house and in my car
> and in my store and in my church
> and in my school and …

That cold Kentucky same, same,
same—keeps falling
like rain in my news.

FLATLINE

Maybe you don't miss ridges
or mountains
or snow melt.
Maybe you never stood
in a holler.
Maybe you don't complain
because even now
there are playgrounds,
clean water,
grocery stores, giant trees,
tall buildings, and skyscrapers
between you
and the horizon,
and you didn't step off your porch
one day and there was nothing left
to block the sun
and everything that used to tower
and stand majestic,
almost mocking the sky
had become a jagged edge,
the new horizon, a troubling flat line.

ORNITHOCRACY

The grackles, doves, jays,
cardinals, and wrens
all watch each other's back.

The ancient differences
between them are much smaller now.
When gathered   they know

that when the hungry pandemic
dashes out of the bushes
or from beneath a parked car,

it will not matter   what color
feathers are left floating
in the wind.

WA-ALAIKUM-SALAAM

Kareem is the first name I think of
as soon as he lands.
The Alcindor of blue jays
—extra-long, athletic and beautifully built.

Feet so strong
he holds sunflower seeds
between his knuckles
while hammering them open
with his massive beak.

The rooster has been calling
revelers home for hours.
Three of the six neighborhood rabbits
amble in the alley green
like teenagers trudging off
to the bus stop or back from the park.

Female wrens hold space
with cardinals of every season,
smaller jays, and bully grackles
obliged to eat from the table scraps
the smaller birds have offered
to the ground.

It's early May.
This quiet morning in the city
drowns out the late night sirens,
blesses us with
this moment of peace.

We offer prayers for this breakfast
—the ratatat tat of woodpeckers
instead of guns.

SHE'S BACK

My nose reacts before my eyes even see her.
She flashed me in a daffodil dress a month ago,
but I knew she was faking and fronting.

It might look like I'm tearing up, but I ain't gon' lie.
As happy as I am to have that cold frosty fish
that moved in last November pack her shit and go,
I ain't missed April all that much.

I mean sure, I'll get to be outside more.
And who don't like a good walk in the park?
But she gonna show off, make a big deal over the smell
of fresh cut grass, noisy-ass birds, flowery colors,
and she won't stop with all the perfume.
I knew she was here before I woke up this morning,
because I already had a headache.

I mean I know I should be happier to see her,
but as nice as she is today, I know
she'll be rumbling and complaining up a storm,
running around in circles, and twisting 'n tearing
shit up before I can say ah-choo.

MULTIVERSE

At first glance in the early light,
I see the Fantastic Four
about to confront
Doctor Doom,
not towering okra plants
in their own green cape
in our backyard.

Instead of The Thing's
rough and Hulk-like physique
ready to bring the pain,
it's our blackberries,
all miniature Grimms,
smothering the wide trellis
for the second time this season.

It is not Reed Richards
stretching to twice the height
of his archetypically beautiful wife
Susan, but our Spartan apple tree
dwarfing it's pollinating companion,
also a shapely Golden Delicious.

And there is no Human Torch
just three different kinds of sunflowers
climbing the morning sky together
—but no less Fantastic.

A KIND OF TAI CHI

For Greg Pape

You always beat me there.
Your reliable all-wheel drive
Subaru with Montana plates,
signaling confidence, calm,
and dependability, immediately
sets the tone in the parking lot.

It seems safer than the old pickup
with its shattered windshield
or the horse that tumbled through it
that I remember from your poems.

By the time we are ready to tee off,
you have reminded me with a smile
and a wink that we are not adversaries.
The golf course is our common enemy.

And every heavy thing we can't carry
for each other for these 18 holes
belongs in the narrow space
between the golf ball and each wooden tee.

Some days we swing with such precision
we dream ourselves on tour.
On others we are happy to blame
even the early morning fog for our poor play,
while we navigate the necessary distance
and direction to the green by memory alone.

We tell our partners that it's just golf,
just a chance to be outside in the fresh air,
but the look in their eyes when we return home
says they know it is a sacred martial art
performed without a dojo,

that the repetitive motion, the quest
for more and more fluidity
and the ever quieting of the mind
is part of everything we need   to be whole.

MARKING TWAIN

the second mark on the line that measured a river's depth,
two fathoms, or twelve feet—safe depth for a steamboat

It's complicated.
Me and the South. Me,
and the land, and the trees.

Whose ever woods these are
are full of hounds, and secrets
and ropes.

These hollers and creeks are all
one American Lit class away from rivers,
and steamboats, and cotton fields.

The difference between hanging burley
from the top rail
and sometimes barely
hanging,
can be as muddy as the difference
between growing up attracted to
any light-skinned girl
with green eyes
and knowing how I got that way.

It's complicated,
me and the South, me
and the land   and the trees.

INSTITUTIONAL LIES

por Oscar

The sanitarium was like a summer home
for him and other residents at the margins.
On his meds meant he floated around
the city like a ghost, unemployable,
at odds with block scheduling,
a slow-motion version of himself
seemingly trapped in another dimension.

Off them meant an *episode* was imminent
and soon he would need to *go away for awhile*
to find his equilibrium, to recalibrate
that look in his eyes that recognized the difference
between a meat cleaver and a butter knife,
his loving mother's face and a chupacabra
or the orderlies coming to take him away.

But I know he ain't *crazy* 'cause
one Christmas holiday,
outside a bank, after being dragged
out of a car, profiled in one glance as stolen,
we were placed three deep on the curb,
hands in non-confrontational positions
surrounded by more guns than police
—and he   didn't   run.

TRAP MUSIC

My sisters found much entertainment
in how fast I would run to escape *weird* Cora.
Just for laughs, they would whisper to her
that she could hug and kiss me, if she caught me.
It wasn't just the kiss.

I was more afraid of the strange grunting noises
she made, her ugly shoe with the extra-large heel,
and a seemingly boneless arm that flopped about
when she ran. I was not mean. Mama commanded
otherwise, but she didn't say I couldn't run, so I did.

Cora called me her boyfriend, which my sisters
exploited, trapping me behind furniture,
chasing me out bedroom windows, her on the scent,
them, pretend aristocrats in a game of fox and hound.

A five-year-old child in a grown woman's body, born
with one leg shorter than the other and a flaccid arm,
who danced and sang badly but with enthusiasm
was funny to them—until it wasn't.

NEIGHBORHOOD WATCH

We don't have guard dogs.
We don't have meddlesome neighbors
peeping out of window curtains.

No bold old ladies unafraid to eyeball
suspicious characters lurking about,
to say "hey, where you going
with them people's grill" or "porch chairs,"
we've just got   cats.

Not the fuzzy kind you want to pick up
and nuzzle, but thug cats
that look you in the eye, prowl, hiss,
dare dogs to bark or for you to chase
them off your warm car.

Thick-legged felines, descended
from cheetahs and panthers,
that we feed by default
because we feed birds
so, they wait in the bushes
until another sparrow lands
and then joins them for dinner.

We have the kind of cats that lead
would-be burglars to the camera blind spots
and unlocked windows,
that leave a muddy trail and scratches
the length of your car just because.

They led the herd of boys passing
through from the park, into our yard,
instructed them to knock the head off
our snowman and run

then signed the work of their
hired guns with paw prints.

We don't have a drug problem
in our neighborhood.

We got cats.

THUNDER ROLLING DOWN THE MOUNTAIN

In Chief Joseph's mountains
in the sacred land of Nimiipuu
when the thunder   storms
you can feel it   in your whole body.
Thunder   rolling down the mountain
again and again like a medicine woman
blessing the air.

When my wife first saw the lake—she cried.
Thunder Rolling Down the Mountain

On our first walkabout we saw the Good Lord Bird
or the biggest woodpecker we've ever seen.
Thunder Rolling Down the Mountain

My son saw his first prairie dog
and was almost touched by a deer.
He chased butterflies, dipped his hand
in the ice-cold stream rushing down to kiss the lake.
He walked the length of a fallen pine without falling off.

Back in Kentucky, there are no snow-capped peaks
in the heart of summer, no mountains forever protected
from rape and pillage,
there aren't more giant trees than stars in the sky
or blue herons and fawns at poetry readings.

He will leave here with more than these memories. He
will leave with new worlds
and this forever prayer, this blessing of words
Thunder   Rolling Down   the Mountain.

FLIGHT LESSONS

for Kumasi

You stare back at me
with my own eyes
and command that I "fix it,"
endowing me with magic powers
to uncrash or unbreak the results
of the Faith you place
in the pretend wings attached
to anything that fits in your hands.

The too-full toy box won't even close,
yet, the veggies on your plate
are your new favorite playthings.

Our Benin brass bell is missing
its clapper. Every single piece of furniture
we own is chipped, scratched or dented.

There isn't a single wall in our house
you haven't kissed with a crayon.

When you were too quiet
you had flooded the bathroom.

Yesterday, I considered trading you
for a puppy, but your mother said, "No."

Today, you attach magnetic triangles
to a square and proudly show us
your "picture of blue mountains."

I let my smile out of its cave,
swell with pride and float
out of the room on new wings.

BIRTH DAY, NO CAKE, NO SONG

Because she could not flush it
with the rest of the placenta,
we buried the amniotic sac
surrounded by a triumvirate
of cowries, eyes facing up
beneath the root ball
of a flowering Anthurium
and not under the Japanese maple
out front for all to see.

Our toddler's heavy-handed caress
broke off one of the brilliant red
blooms earlier in the day
and made it the only easy decision
to make.

We placed this new being
in the stairwell
opposite the picture window
that bears witness to each
sun rise, below the site
of the bloody mess we made,
to remind us
during our many ups and downs,
of what we've lost,
of what we've gained.

I cooked a late breakfast
including her favorite fried potatoes,
—but could not find the courage
to offer her the eggs.

RIDING SHOTGUN

for Sheldon

Traveling from the calm warm water
and sand in Ocho Rios
to her birthplace in Clarendon,
we take the old road through Fern Gully,
which crawls sloth-like between
moss-covered rocks and beneath ferns
so thick they blot out the sun.

When the throat of this ancient flora maze
eventually opens, we are coughed out
alongside a shallow river that follows
the movement of the road like
a dancehall queen winding her hips
just so on the quick and the slow songs.

Creeping over a cement spill
pretending to be a bridge, the road high-steps,
bobs and weaves, then drops down
into the splits so quickly
I almost taste my breakfast, again.

I can tell by her brother's wicked grin
as he points out the straight new road
in the distance that this is the part in the movie
where the locals eat fire ants,
wrestle a crocodile, or push the city slicker
off a three-story waterfall.

My eyes stop following the road
and oncoming traffic at my beseeching
and I undizzy myself by staring at the
tree-covered mountains in the distance.
They are far enough away

to make me believe every green thing
doesn't want to rip the road out from under us.

The Six Flags attraction continues to wind
and climb and double back on itself
until it feels like we are looking down from heaven
at the prototype Garden of Eden
with a miles-long asphalt serpent
that had me praying at every hairpin turn.

Then I smile when I finally understand.
This is just a crazy Jamaican ritual to see
if I am worthy of his sister.
I reach back, caress her hand,
study the quiet and hope
in her face and decide to just enjoy the view.

CUMULO NIMBUS

When a warm front settles in,
music drifts down from her study,
dances across the hardwood,
and fills up the entire downstairs.

Her voluminous songs light the oven,
top off her wine glass and shine
so bright it almost blinds the boy.

She can don a pretty skirt,
head out for a stroll and heat up
the whole block.
Anybody lucky enough to see her smile
thinks about Jamaica, blue seas
and white sand all day.

But thunder in her heels can rumble
down the stairs and through the walls.
When her storm clouds move in
you can feel the barometric
pressure change in your bones.

These are good days to fall into a book,
catch up on busywork or daydream about
how much I like to play   in the rain.

SELFIE: TALLY

> "You don't get to be old bein' no fool."
> —Richard Pryor

I've been looking at my gray hair all wrong.
My chin is a scoreboard. Each white wizen stalk
is a regal ribbon representing a mistake I've made

and was fortunate enough to learn from.
The remaining proud black banners huddled together
and trying to hide, are all the blunders I made

and then multiplied by failing to discern the lesson.
The path to wisdom is not to not make mistakes,
but to always be smart enough   to learn from them.

A POEM OF GRATITUDE

after Yusef Komunyakaa

Thank you love, for him, for today, for the not-so-secret smile
I'm wearing now. Thank you for voicing your pleasure without
restraint for making space for me to voice mine. Thank you for
pushing me through our discomfort, for demanding honesty,
trust, respect. I want those same things too. Thanks for being
naked in the daylight, bearing witness to our softness our exposed
bellies smiling at each other. Thank you for not hiding. For not
trying to hide. For reminding me that if I'm paying close attention
I don't have to wait for permission to touch.

ACKNOWLEDGMENTS

Grateful acknowledgements to the editors of the following journals and anthologies in which some of these poems first appeared, some under different titles: *The Brownies Book: A Love Letter to Black Families*, *The Louisville Review*, *Troublesome Rising: A Thousand-Year Flood in Eastern Kentucky*, *The Forum Magazine*, *The Art of Revising Poetry*, and *The About Place Journal: Center of Gravity Issue*.

"Neoteric Kama No Sutra" also appeared in the *Academy of American Poets* website, "Poem-a-Day" as part of a month of love sonnets curated by Patricia Smith.

Gratitude to Mark Johnson whose vision for the Artists' Village provided the space in which so many of these poems were born, for Katerina Stoykova and her endless support, for Shauna Melissa Morgan, the perfect first reader and editor my sleep-challenged, grasshopper brain could ever have, and the many friends, students, colleagues, and fellow artists and writers who live and work in community with us as we continue to chase these words.

ABOUT THE AUTHOR

Multidisciplinary artist and educator, Frank X Walker, is the first African American writer to be named Kentucky Poet Laureate. He is the author of the children's book, *A is for Affrilachia*, and eleven collections of poetry, including *Turn Me Loose: The Unghosting of Medgar Evers*, which was awarded the NAACP Image Award for Poetry and the Black Caucus American Library Association Honor Award. Voted one of the most creative professors in the south, Walker coined the term "Affrilachia" and co-founded the Affrilachian Poets. He serves as Professor of Creative Writing and African American and Africana Studies at the University of Kentucky.

OTHER BOOKS BY FRANK X WALKER

Eclipsing a Nappy New Millennium, Editor (1997)

Affrilachia (2000)

Buffalo Dance: The Journey of York (2004)

Black Box (2006)

America! What's My Name?, Editor (2007)

When Winter Come: The Ascension of York (2008)

Isaac Murphy: I Dedicate This Ride (2010)

Turn Me Loose: The Unghosting of Medgar Evers (2013)

About Flight (2015)

Affrilachian Sonnets (2016)

Ink Stains & Watermarks: New and Uncollected Poems (2017)

Last Will, Last Testament (2019)

Masked Man, Black (2020)

A is for Affrilachia (2023)